Becoming Responsible Learners

Becoming Responsible Learners

Learners Strategies for positive classroom management

Mark Collis & Joan Dalton

Heinemann
Portsmouth, NH

HEINEMANN EDUCATIONAL BOOKS INC.
361 Hanover Street Portsmouth, NH 03801
Offices and agents throughout the world

ISBN 0 435 08568 9

Published simultaneously in the United States
in 1990 by Heinemann
and in Australia by
Eleanor Curtain Publishing
2 Hazeldon Place
South Yarra 3141

Production by Sylvana Scannapiego
Island Graphics
Designed by Sarn Potter
Cover design by David Constable
Photographs by J. Ridgers
Typeset by Trade Graphics Pty Ltd
Printed in Australia by
Impact Printing

CONTENTS

ACKNOWLEDGEMENTS

This book is a revised and expanded edition of a project which grew from an initiative of the Tasmanian Early Childhood Senior Staff Association (Northern Region) and was made possible through the support and expertise of senior Education Department personnel, in particular Margaret Bartkevicius (Superintendent) and Beverley Richardson (Student Services Director). Most of all it occurred because of the way in which successful teachers shared their classroom practice with us. We are indeed each others' best resources.

CONTRIBUTING TEACHERS

Nadia Ambroz
Sharon Ansell
Stuart Beveridge
Rosalie Boxhall
Elizabeth Brient
Catherine Britton
Kathleen Brophy
Margaret Carey
Sharyn Cook
Tammi Cooper
Elizabeth Daly
Andrea Dare
Stephen Davidson
Jenny Dewis
Margaret Dixon
Liz Elliot

Helen Fox
Kerryn Gabel
Mary-Ann Griggs
Leanne Grimditch
Rachel Hall
Denise Hay
Jenni Howlett
Margaret Johns
Christine Landles
Cathy Lathey
Peg Leary
Denise Lyons
Vicki Mackrill
Trudi Mitchell
Janette Moore
Margaret Morice

Wendy Nicks
Maree O'Byrne
Anne Palmer
Margaret Pearce
Jo Richelme
Julie Rundle
Maria San Segundo
Bev Scolyer
Bev Shadbolt
Kathryn Targett
Shireen Thomas
Debbie Turner
Mary-Ann Warner
Elizabeth Whittle
Lesa Woodward

Sincere thanks to the Principal, staff and children of Waverley Primary School and Perth Primary School for allowing our photographer to record some of the excellent work being done in their schools.

ABOUT BECOMING RESPONSIBLE

Ideas for good stories always come from somewhere. The idea for this story, *Becoming Responsible Learners*, grew from an initiative of a Senior Staff Association in northern Tasmania, Australia. These early childhood educators were concerned about the seemingly growing incidence of children with behaviour difficulties and the resultant effects on children and teachers. An ensuing research investigation supported this, but revealed one curious fact. In some schools where there were known to be such children, the teachers did not report them as being of concern. This raised two important questions:

- What were these teachers doing to help children function effectively and behave in positive ways?
- How might we as researchers find this out, and share their practical strategies with other teachers?

As colleagues, we have a strong belief in the power of peer learning. Because of this, we brought together fifty teachers who had been identified as working very successfully with children who have behaviour difficulties. In small teams, they shared ideas and documented their classroom practices. What emerged showed very clearly that these teachers are effective with *all* children, and that they share a consistent belief — a belief that the very best way to prepare children for the future and to have them become successful learners is to help them *learn* to take increasing responsibility for their learning and behaviour. As one teacher put it 'you can't *make* kids behave — they choose to behave in certain ways. But I can influence them. And the most powerful way I can influence them is to help them become responsible choice-makers, to take progressive responsibility for themselves and their actions'.

This teacher is wise. She and the other successful teachers we worked with believe what is strongly supported by academic research.

When children have a stake in their learning, when they own responsibility for that learning and when they feel a sense of increasing control over themselves and their actions, powerful things happen. They become more committed to their learning and so are motivated to learn. Their basic needs are more likely to be met — they learn to use their personal power constructively and to make informed choices. They take more conscious control of their learning and so they learn more effectively.

As they become autonomous learners, they grow in self-confidence and in their belief in themselves. As they develop this stronger sense of inner direction they are more able to work with others and to build healthy relationships in an interdependent, rather than dependent way. These abilities will be critical in a future world of rapid and accelerating

vii

change and complexity, an amazing explosion of information and choices, and an increasing need for people and nations to work together.

Successful teachers are not only distinguished by their belief that children need to work this way, but by their ability to translate this belief into classroom practice. Our observations suggest that it is their flexible, empowering style of leadership in the classroom that is a key factor in enabling them to do this.

Classroom leadership styles

Teacher ownership & control	Shared ownership & control	Child ownership & control
'Do as I say' 'I'll decide'	'Do as we agree' 'Let's decide together'	'Do as you want' 'You decide'

The empowering style of shared ownership provides the base from which these teachers operate, and they are able to move to less or more restrictive modes according to the context and the children's needs.

A sole focus, or too early a focus, on child ownership and control can mean too many choices and too few limits, resulting in confusion and insecurity. In this kind of setting children learn, 'I have all the power' and often lack the skills for responsible behaviour and learning. This is particularly true for children who have behaviour difficulties.

However, if the dominant mode is strong teacher ownership and control and all the power resides with the teacher, children may learn to meet their power needs in non-productive ways. Importantly, they also learn that others are responsible for their behaviour and learning.

The shared ownership style is empowering in several important ways. It is a style which

- helps children learn to take increasing responsibility for themselves
- allows for progressive ownership by children as they are able
- provides opportunity and structure so that children learn appropriate skills
- recognises the need for children to see themselves as part of a broader team.

Its foundation is negotiation, cooperation and shared problem solving. Children learn 'I am responsible for me, and we can all make a contribution to each others' learning'.

Teachers who work this way are able to build a classroom environment where children feel a sense of security and belonging, where their needs for power and freedom are met constructively, and where learning is more fun. They acknowledge the strong links between behavioural learning and curriculum learning and use consistent ways of helping children learn responsibility for both. Importantly, these teachers recognise the value of their own peer support and are able to share responsibility at school level. They are not only committed to helping children become responsible learners, they are on-going learners themselves.

This book is a tribute to the many teachers who have shared their rich store of strategies with us — it challenges you to think about the links between learning and behaviour, and provides ideas that have worked for practising teachers. Use this book as a resource — talk about the ideas with colleagues, try some of them out, and further develop and share your own.

Mark Collis   Joan Dalton

1

CREATING A POSITIVE CLASSROOM ENVIRONMENT

Early morning is a good time to visit Helen's classroom. Children arrive up to half an hour before regular bell time and parents often visit with their children during this period. Kylie proudly shows her father the maths challenge she has been working on and Josh's mother helps her son work through his spelling. Wendy and two friends snuggle into a beanbag with Wendy's mother, as they enjoy a favourite book together.

Children move quickly into their 'set' workjobs — spelling and maths, and then into optional activities. Helen uses this time to welcome each child, to provide individual or small group assistance and to talk with parents who are visiting. The atmosphere is busy but calm, and the displays around the classroom reflect the culture of the classroom. There is a sign saying "Welcome to the Years One and Two team' above a chart with 26 photographs of all the children in the class. Helen's is included as one of the team. Another sign reads 'Our Rules' with four positive statements underneath. Yet another list, 'Ways we help each other'.

At around 9.15am, Helen asks the children to pack up and come together on the mat. She notices Mark is not packing the Lego away and moves to him, saying 'Mark, see how Tim is packing the Lego into this special box. That's what you need to do before joining us on the mat'. As Mark joins the group she says 'Thank you Mark. We appreciate you packing the Lego away. It helps to keep our room tidy'. To the children Helen says, 'Lets have a look at what Annette has been making — that's really unusual Annette — no one else has thought of doing it that way.'

This glimpse of Helen's class may seem at face value a simple picture, however Helen is employing some powerful beliefs and principles in working with children.

Successful teachers like Helen believe children's behaviour is learned and that it is learned through interaction with their environment. The kind of classroom environment that children with behaviour difficulties experience is critical to the development of appropriate ways to behave.

These key beliefs enable effective teachers to work at building a classroom environment
- where children feel a sense of physical and emotional security
- where children can expect consistency in their daily school lives
- where both experience and feedback help children to behave appropriately
- where teachers model positive communication and behaviour, and encourage children to do the same.

HELP CHILDREN TO FEEL SECURE

Spend some time establishing consistent routines and procedures:
'What are the ways you can get help if I am busy with other people?'
'What must you do before going onto a new activity?'
'How many children do you think can use the painting area at one time?'

Ensure that children are clear about the consequences of not following procedures:
Teacher: 'In our classroom we pack away things we've used before going onto something else.'
Johnny: 'No! Don't want to pack up the stupid blocks.'
Teacher: 'Johnny, you can choose to pack-up, or you can choose to sit here and not take part in our next thing which is a story.'

Develop a shared set of class rules
- Initiate class discussion:
  'How would you like other people to treat you in our room?'
- Try to list children's suggestions in positive ways
  Child: 'We don't break our friend's things.'
  Teacher: 'That's right we care for other people's property.'
- Help children to evaluate their suggestions:
  'Is that fair to everyone?'
  'Which rules do you think are the most important for us to remember?'

Saffron and Olivia are outside working.
Only 2 people to be outside at one time so you will need to choose something else to do until they come in.

Rules of our classroom

In our classroom we:

. co-operate and help one another

. listen to others so they will listen to us

. behave in a sensible way

. remember that everyone has the right to be able to work without being disturbed

. look after our books and equipment

. take responsibility for cleaning up the area we play and work in.

1. Work quietly, neatly and be sensible.

2. Co-operate with everyone and care for them.

3. Clean up your own mess and put things back where you found them.

4. Look after everything.

5. Put your name on all your work before you start.

6. Only one person speaks at a time.

7. Leave other people's things alone.

8. The storeroom is for teachers only.

'How could we make one rule out of these three?'
- Keep rules simple, few in number and display them where children can see them as needed.
- Revisit rules from time to time:
  'Let's look at our rules and see if they are working for us.'
  'Which things are we doing well?'
  'What do we need to work on?'
  'How can we show care for other people's property?'

Be available at consistent times

'I like to be in class half-an-hour before school starts. I find it is a good time to talk personally with Leigh — he often comes in if he's upset about something.'

'Jenny knows that I am going to conference with her before playtime. It helps her manage her learning time.'

FOSTER A SENSE OF BELONGING

Use the language of unity

'It's up to *us* to solve that problem.'
'*We* need to do these things by playtime.'

Make use of welcoming signs

'Welcome to our class. These are the people who live here.'

Encourage whole class contributions

- Work on special projects, such as giant jigsaws, organising grandparents' day, class murals.
- Set some common class goals. 'Our goal this week is to return all our library books on time.'

Help parents to feel they belong

'That's a terrific new bag that Jessica has. Did you buy it during the holidays?'

'I'd love to have you help with our language programme this year.'

- Keep a parent notice board on display.

ACCENT THE POSITIVES

Encourage children in what we say

'I like to give children feedback on what it is we value ... and understand how this value helps everyone.'

'Jane, we appreciate your packing these blocks away. It helps to keep our room tidy.' (reminding of common group values)

'Thank you for sitting that way Darren. Now we can begin our story.' (learning to be part of the group)

'Oh, Mary, thank you! We can always count on you to remember when it's time to go to the library.' (valuing self)

'Isn't it interesting how we all have different ideas. When we share them with each other, we all learn more!' (valuing difference)

'Mario, no one else has thought of doing it that way, that's unusual!' (accepting and valuing difference)

'We seem to have different ideas on that, but everyone is entitled to their own opinion.' (accepting difference)

Turn negatives into positives
'We don't shout in our room, do we Miss Gee?'
'That's right, Mark, we use quiet voices.'

Encourage children in what we do
• Use positive models to encourage children.
  'Neville, see how Tim is packing the blocks into that special cupboard. That's what you need to do before starting your next workjob.'
• Be positive in non-verbal ways: smile, nod, wink, shake hands, give a quick hug.

Put it down on paper

• Give written feedback to every child over time.

• Provide written feedback to parents, for example on notes, cards, or use video.

USE AN ASSERTIVE INTERPERSONAL STYLE

Cue children by using their name prior to talking with them

'Vanessa and Kylie — you have five minutes left to finish off — then it will be packing up time.'

Provide appropriate non-verbal messages

• Establish eye contact before giving messages — be sensitive to different cultural values here.

• Work at children's physical level when talking personally.

• Move *to* children to communicate personally, rather than correct or talk to a child across a classroom.

Wendy is at the story desk and continually talking to others who are intent on writing. Mrs Thomas moves across, kneels down beside Wendy and enquires in a quiet voice 'Wendy, I notice a lot of talking going on here. What are our class rules for working at the writing desk?' ...
(Problem solving process starts here ...)

Develop personalised ways of cueing children

Sally has difficulty maintaining concentration on her activity. Ms Lane finds that, as she moves around the room, a simple touch on Sally's shoulder helps Sally and encourages her to continue concentrating without drawing her attention away from the task.

BUILD INTERPERSONAL SKILLS IN CHILDREN

All children need to develop positive relations with others. Many children with behaviour difficulties will lack the basic skills they need to enable this to happen. Just as we need to plan for children's academic growth, we also need to plan for their inter-personal growth.

Take Alex for instance.

Alex has been asked to work with three other children on a small group learning challenge. He moves quickly to the group table and begins work with his group. Alex frequently interjects with comments such as 'Hey, what about ...' or 'That's stupid!', without waiting for others to finish. In fact, Jodi doesn't get the chance to contribute with Alex present.

It is important to build from where Alex is at, and look at what he needs to learn to do. In that way the teacher will be able to help him.

Alex can:	Alex needs to learn:
move to a group	to take turns
stay with a group	to use other's names
begin tasks	to encourage others
stay on task	
contribute to the group	

To help Alex learn to take turns, we could:

- Have Alex work initially with a partner rather than a large group, assigning roles of 'listener' and 'talker', then swapping over.
- Make use of a physical object, for example, a small shell, and pass it to group members as it is their turn to talk.
- Have a parent or other adult sit with the group and cue turn-taking. (As with all successful parent participation in classroom programmes, take time to build parent skills first.)

Children's awareness of ways to encourage others could be raised in this way

After talking to the children about why it's important to encourage everyone to have a go, ask them what are some of the things they can say and do to encourage others. Together build up a list like this.

ENCOURAGING OTHERS

Things we can say
What do you think Vicki?
That's a good idea Johnny
That's terrific Jill

Things we can do
Smile
Look at the person

Let them know that you will be looking for the ways they encourage each other.

ORGANISE THE PHYSICAL ENVIRONMENT

Children with behaviour difficulties need a physical environment where space, materials and procedures are clearly laid out and understood.

Use space effectively

- Create spaces for different kinds of activities. Consider spaces for whole class meetings, small group activities, space for individual work or being alone, spaces for quiet/noisy work and messy/careful activities.
- Set clear boundaries using such things as carpets, rugs, furniture, drapes, corrugated cardboard …
- Design spaces to meet paticular needs, for example, a three-sided learning carrel to enhance concentration, a mini-trampoline for energy release.

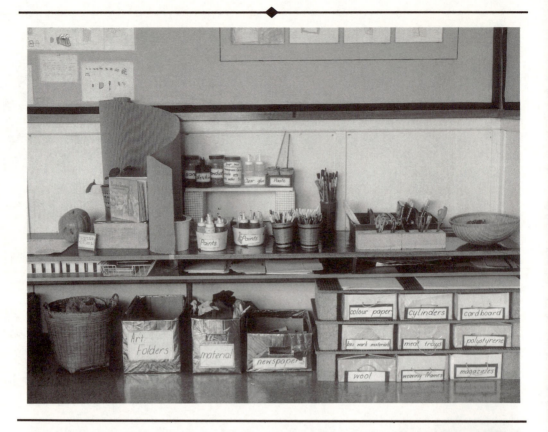

Organise materials systematically

- Arrange materials so that they are accessible to children, for example, open shelving rather than closed cupboards.
- Make available a variety of learning centres and materials, for example, sand and water, construction, art materials ...

Display visual reminders

- Label spaces and materials clearly.
- Reinforce procedures to be followed pictorially or in writing.

Effective teachers deliberately and consciously create a positive classroom environment as an integral part of helping children to become responsible learners. It lays a critical foundation from which they can enhance self-motivation and positive attitudes to learning. It provides the context for building skills necessary to help children assume increasing responsibility for both their learning and behaviour.

2
DEVELOPING RESPONSIBILITY FOR LEARNING

In Mary-Ann's classroom, Andrew has brought his budgerigar to show his classmates. 'What questions would you like to ask Andrew about "Charlie"?' Mary-Ann asks the children. Andrew deftly takes charge of the discussion as questions follow — Mary-Ann simply listens. Then she comments. 'Charlie certainly creates a lot of interest — I wonder if you'd like to make up a learning challenge around Charlie for the children, Andrew?'

'Yep' says Andrew, 'They've asked me a lot of questions about his colors, so I think we'll put Charlie on the art table, get out the brown paper and pastels, and people can use Charlie as the focus point for some art observations.' Andrew is five years of age and in Prep/1 class.

Of the children she asks, 'When you were talking with Andrew, what was I doing?' 'Listening' is the unanimous reply. Mary-Ann draws from children why they think listening is important, then asks, 'What can we do and say when people are talking to us to show that we are listening?' Together they build a list of specific things on the blackboard that show this. John, a lively six-year-old says 'I'd say — I didn't know that before you told me,' and Mary-Ann adds that to the list.

'While you're doing your workjobs,' Mary-Ann explains, 'my job will be to notice how you're listening to each other, and to give you some feedback on that. We'll share how we've done just before lunch.'

Mary-Ann models a strong belief that children develop a commitment to learning when they share the ownership of that learning. For children with behaviour difficulties this ownership is essential.

The personal insights we can gain from Mary-Ann's style of interaction in the classroom are part of her broad plan for helping children become responsible learners. A way of viewing her style is to look at a classroom leadership continuum:

Classroom Leadership: learning

Teacher Ownership	Shared Ownership	Child Ownership
• strong teacher control	• shared control	• strong child control
• 'I decide what you will do'	• 'Let's decide together'	• 'You decide what you will do'
• external control based on authority	• the teacher invites:	• internal control based on self-direction
• teacher makes — decisions	— input	• 'I'm responsible for my learning'
— choices	— negotiation	• children are independent of the teacher
• teacher is responsible for learning	— responsibility	
• children are dependent on the teacher	— co-operation	
	and helps children learn the appropriate skills for becoming responsible learners	
	• children are learning both independence and interdependence	
	• 'I am responsible for my learning and I care about the learning of others'	

Successful teachers, like Mary-Ann, can use all of these leadership styles in a flexible manner, according to the situation and children's learning needs. The 'shared ownership' style, however, is the most powerful way to build commitment to learning, and importantly, is the base from which to help children *learn* the skills necessary for responsible learning.

Effective teachers help children to take increasing responsibility for their own learning:

• by teaching them the skills involved in learning how-to-learn

• by providing opportunities for risk-taking and time for feedback and reflection

- by contracting to maximise the chance of both challenge and success for all children
- by negotiating to help meet individual needs

NEGOTIATE WITH CHILDREN

Make decisions about what may be negotiated

Decide whether negotiation will be with individuals, small groups or the whole class. Any or all of these may be negotiated:
- learning goals
- content of what is to be learned
- how the learning will be approached and undertaken
- when the learning will take place
- what the outcome/product will be
- how learning will be assessed

Be assertive in helping the child to understand what is negotiable and what is not

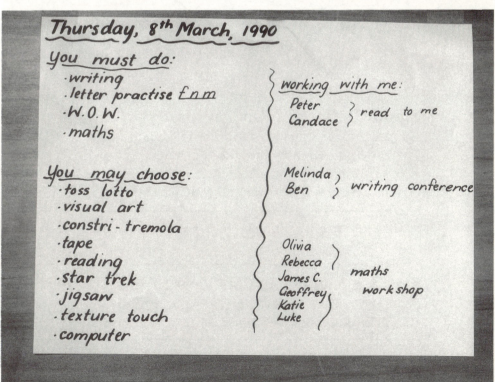

Thursday, 8th March, 1990

You must do:
- writing
- letter practise f n m
- W.O.W.
- maths

You may choose:
- toss lotto
- visual art
- constri - tremola
- tape
- reading
- star trek
- jigsaw
- texture touch
- computer

working with me:

Peter
Candace } read to me

Melinda
Ben } writing conference

Olivia
Rebecca
James C.
Geoffrey
Katie
Luke } maths workshop

'Can I do my measurement card now?'

'No Mark. This is the time we *all* have quiet reading. When do you think would be a better time to do it?'

'Your letter must be finished today, but you may do it before or after lunch.'

Involve children in decision-making

Use a problem-solving process with children in negotiating learning needs. This kind of strategy helps children to increasingly share in determining what they already know, what they need to learn, which learning experiences will meet their needs, and how those learnings will be assessed.

A PROCESS FOR MEETING LEARNING NEEDS*

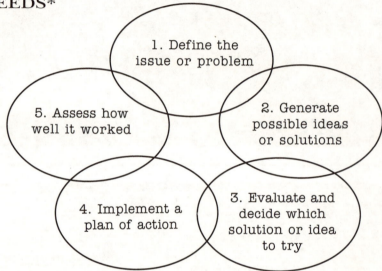

Step 1: Define the issue/needs

A critical first step is to identify what the child already can do.

'What do you already know about that?'

'Let's list the things you have learned about … '

'What are the things you need to learn?'

> Give children as much help as needed at any step of the process.

Step 2: Generate possible ideas for meeting needs

'What are all the ways we might explore that?'

'Let's think of some more ideas for working on that.'

> Generate, don't evaluate at this stage.

*See Chapter 5: A Problem-solving Process

Step 3: Evaluate and decide which idea to try

'Which question will you choose to explore?'
'Which activity will help you learn the most?'
'Let's look at those ideas again, and consider each one carefully.'

> Go back to previous steps where necessary.

Step 4: Implement a plan of action

'How will we go about finding out?'
'Let's make a plan to make sure you achieve your goals … '
'What are the things we will need to consider/plan for?'
'Let's review your learning contract at the end of the week.'

> Make sure the plan is clear and able to be achieved.

Step 5: Assess how well it worked

'How will we know and show that we've been successful?
Let's list three things to help us judge.'

◆

'You certainly understand this part well — what do you need to work on now?'

Provide feedback to the child and opportunity for child self-assessment.

Help children to consider all aspects of their learning:

CONTENT What to learn	'Which two learning centres will you use today?' 'What things do you already know about? What things do you need to know? Which of these will you choose?'
PROCESS How to learn	'How will you do this activity today: by yourself? with a partner? with a small group? with me?' 'How will you work on learning that: using a tape recorder and headphones, talking with a friend, or playing a game?' 'How can we find out about ... ?'
PRODUCT Presenting learnings Assessing	'How will you present your work: talking, writing, making, drawing?' 'How will you share what you've learned? — with me, a friend, or with the whole class?' 'What will help us to decide on how we've done?'
TIME When learning is to be done	'You may do your story first or use the Maths Challenge Centre'. 'These are the things that need to be done — you may choose the order in which you do them.'
PLACE Where the learning takes place	'You may work on that on the floor or at a table.' 'You can finish that in our room today, in the library this afternoon, or at home tonight.' 'Where do you think you could work on that in order to get it finished?'

ESTABLISH CLEAR GOALS

Create awareness of the need to set goals

'Our goal in maths this morning is … because …'

Set clear expectations and explain why

'These are our learning challenges today — why do you think we do these things? What are the things we learn?'

Work out assessment criteria

'How will we know if we are successful in reaching our goal? Let's list two things to help us judge that.'

Progressively involve children in goal-setting

'These are the tasks I'd like you to do today, Ben. How do you think you'll manage them?' (teacher direction with limited child input)

'Let's talk about the workjobs you did yesterday, Ben, and work out some new goals for today.' (joint negotiation between teacher and child)

'Miss Carter, my goal today is to finish my story.'

'Ben, what workjob goals have you set this morning?' (child initiated goal-setting)

Ensure that goals are realistic and achievable for children

'Judi's goal is to learn names of major types of transport. To achieve this goal she is making a class mural using magazine cut outs.'

NAME .... WEEK ....

MY GOALS THIS WEEK ....

....

....

To help achieve my goals I will ....

....

Mrs Jones will help me by ....

....

When I have finished ....

....

TEACHER .... STUDENT ....

PARENT ....

'Sharon and Theo need a complex challenge. Their goal is to investigate the need for a public bus service along High Street. Billy finds it difficult to complete learning tasks. Today we will make each task very short and give him feedback after each one.'

HELP CHILDREN MANAGE TIME

Set clear time limits
'These two things must be finished by playtime.'

Help children to think about how much time workjobs will take
'How much time do you think you will need for that?'
'This can be done ... or ... When do you think would be the best time?'

Help children to plan out their time constructively
'Which one will you do first? second ...? third...?'
'Which part will take the longest?'

Make use of written plans and timelines

My time plan — PROJECT 'SPIDERS' — Jodi

DATE	CHOOSE TOPIC	LIST QUESTIONS	FIND INFORMATION	ORGANISE INFORMATION	PREPARE TO SHARE	SHARE

Chris — MONDAY

I have
- SHARED A BOOK WITH A FRIEND ☐
- WORKED AT MY MATHS ☐
- WORKED ON MY WRITING ☐

MAKE CHILDREN ACCOUNTABLE FOR THEIR CHOICES

Introduce choices progressively, limiting them at first
'For maths today you have two choices ... or ...'
'You may use our learning centres or work on your research when you have finished reading.'
'You can make it using clay, boxes or cut and paste.'

Involve children increasingly in choice-making
'What art materials will you use in making your tower?'

'When you finish these workjobs, what activities would you like to do?'

Set positive expectations of consequences

Consider the difference between:

'Johnny, if you don't finish this maths game you won't be in time to hear our new story.'

'Johnny, when you finish that maths game you'll be able to hear our new story.'

Relate choices made directly to consequences

'Mandy, it's almost playtime and I notice you haven't started your workjob. You can *choose* to do it now, or you can *choose* to do it during playtime.'

Follow consequences through consistently

'Mandy, you chose not to finish your workjob this morning. As we agreed, I'm going to give you the *opportunity* to finish it during the first five minutes of playtime.'

'Mandy, thanks for choosing to do that reading. It means we can all enjoy our new game together.'

It's important to relate choices to the consequences of behaviour, and also to choose consequences that we can live with.

BUILD IN FEEDBACK AND REFLECTION TIME

Give children feedback on their learning

'I noticed you went about doing it in this particular way ...'

'I like the way you used different materials to create that effect.'

'I noticed you allowed enough time today for each activity — well done.'

Have children give feedback to each other

'Let's talk about how each person helped the group today.'

'Jamie helped us by working on the drawings for our story.'

Encourage reflection at whole class, small group and individual levels

'How do you feel about the way we have all worked today?'

'Share with a friend the best thing you have done today.'

'Decide one thing you worked well on today ... What do you think helped that to happen?'

'Which techniques would you like to try again?'

DEVELOP ASSESSMENT AND EVALUATION SKILLS

Relate assessment back to goal-setting to identify what has been achieved

'Let's look at your goals for today and see how successful you've been.'

Encourage children to self-assess

'What did you learn from that task today?'

'Was that a good choice? Why or why not?'

'How well did you meet your goals?'

'Which things did you do well?'

'What could you do to make it better next time?'

'What do you need to work on?'

Foster peer assessment

'How do you think Martine met that challenge today?'

'Let's check each other's answers and we'll talk about the ones we got different answers for.'

Introduce record keeping procedures gradually, so that children develop skills in this area

Consider the use of individual and small group folders containing work samples, self-assessments, progress cards, and so on.

Invite input on the classroom programme

'It's hard to make time to look at everybody's work. What suggestions can you make?'

'We've had a lot of use from the reading trolley. What changes would you like to see so that we can continue to enjoy it?'

Effective teachers take the time and provide the guidance necessary to help children learn a range of skills necessary to becoming autonomous learners. Importantly, they focus on consistency of approach in helping children to develop responsibility for learning and responsibility for behaviour.

3

DEVELOPING RESPONSIBILITY FOR BEHAVIOUR

◆

The children in Steve's Grade 6 are busily working in teams spread around the room. Above the general hum of the classroom come two voices raised in argument from near the video recorder. Turning around from his conferencing group Steve sees Tanya and Troy, both children renowned for temper outbursts, having a tug'o'war with the video's remote control.

Steve moves quickly across the room.

'Tanya … Troy put the remote down, gently,' he orders in a quiet but firm voice. Troy lets go immediately leaving the remote in the sole custody of Tanya. She promptly lifts it above her head and hurls it at the wall. As it splinters she yells,

'I hate you, I hate this f…ing place and I hate all the kids in it!' and stares defiantly at Steve.

Steve feels the blood rush to his face and the skin tighten on the back of his neck. His first impulse is to hit back — he is angry. In a strained voice Steve orders Tanya and Troy to sit at the opposite ends of an octagonal table.

'I'm too angry to talk now,' says Steve, 'sit here until we all calm down enough to talk sensibly about this!' He then moves back to his conferencing group and takes a few deep breaths.

Five minutes go by before Steve stands up again. He moves around the class pausing momentarily to give feedback to a group that had been sitting near Tanya and Troy.

'Thanks for ignoring Tanya and Troy's behaviour — they calmed down really quickly because you ignored them.'

Eventually Steve makes his way back to the octagonal table and sits down beside Tanya. He turns to Troy and says,

'Troy, go on with your contract job and I'll see you after Tanya and I have had a talk.'

Troy nods and moves away.

Turning toward Tanya, Steve says, 'Before we start talking about this Tanya, you must understand that I will be contacting your parents about what happened — remember one of our class rules is that when equipment like this is broken parents are called.' He draws a little closer to her and says softly, 'O.K.?'

Tanya looks away sullenly but nods in resignation.

'Right, tell me what happened', Steve inquires.

'Nothin'',' retorts Tanya's, eyes diverted away from Steve.

In a voice just audible to Tanya, Steve asserts, 'Well this is what I saw Tanya. I saw Troy and you fighting.'

'Troy wouldn't let me have a turn and he called me a name,' Tanya sidetracks.

'O.K. That's what Troy did and I'll be talking with him in a moment. What did you do?'

There is a brief pause that seems like an age to Steve before Tanya offers,

'I broke the remote control.'

'What happened then?' Steve inquires softly.

'Then I yelled,' says Tanya now looking Steve in the eyes.

'So we've got two problems. You broke the video's remote control and we can't edit the videotape without it; and you got angry and stopped other people in the class from concentrating on what they were learning — right?'

Tanya nods in assent.

'Let's work on one problem at a time. What can we do about the remote control?' Steve asks.

'I could fix it', Tanya offers.

'That's one idea, can you think of another?' prompts Steve.

I could pay for a new one, or take it home for Mum or Dad to fix', the ideas come more quickly.

'Have you any more ideas Tanya?' Steve adds after a little pause.

'No', replies Tanya.

'So we have three ideas. You could fix it yourself. You could pay for a new one or you could ask your parents to help you fix or replace it,' Steve summarises. 'Which of those ideas do you think you'll be able to do?'

'Well, I don't think I could fix it myself', Tanya says looking at the pieces scattered across the floor. 'And I haven't got enough money to buy another one.' Tanya pauses and looks down at her toes avoiding any eye contact with Steve.

'So which idea will work for you', prompts Steve.

'I could ask Mum and Dad to help me fix it or get another one I suppose', she answers reluctantly.

'So asking Mum and Dad to help you fix it or replace it will best solve our problem of the broken remote?' Steve queries.

'Yeah', Tanya replies a little more confidently.

'Well you talk to your Mum and Dad tonight and we'll get together tomorrow and see how you went. Remember I'll be talking to them this afternoon so they'll be expecting you to talk about what happened today pretty soon after you get home, right?' Steve adds smiling.

Tanya looks up and smiles faintly, 'Right', she affirms.

'O.K. That still leaves the problem of getting angry. Lets leave that till next Thursday and tackle that one when we've got a little more time', Steve smiles.

Steve knows that children learn to take responsibility for their behaviour just as they learn to take responsibility for their own learning. He knows that when children learn to accept this responsibility then positive behaviour change will occur.

The way Steve interacts with children in his classroom gives us a picture of how children learn to behave in responsible ways. A way of understanding this picture more deeply is to look at the leadership continuum:

Classroom Leadership: behaviour

Teacher Ownership	*Shared Ownership*	*Child Ownership*
• strong teacher control	• shared control	• strong child control
• 'I decide what you will do'	• 'let's decide together'	• 'you decide what you will do'
• external control based on authority	• the teacher invites :	• internal control based on self-direction/discipline
• teacher makes decisions	– negotiation/input	• 'I'm responsible for how I behave'
• teacher is responsible for behaviour	– responsibility	• children are independent of teacher
children are dependent on the teacher	– co-operation and helps children learn skills	
	• for behaving appropriately children are learning both independence and interdependence	
	• 'I am responsible for my behaviour and I care about the behaviour of others'	

Effective teachers like Steve use all of these leadership styles in a flexible manner, according to the situation and children's particular needs. However, the 'shared ownership' style is the most powerful way to build commitment and, importantly, is the base from which to help children learn the skills necessary to behave responsibly.

Teachers who are successful with children who have behaviour difficulties work at changing behaviour in the following ways:

- they are not sidetracked by excuses for behaviour

- they deal with conflict in a calm and positive manner

- they empower the child with the resources necessary for change.

RESPOND IMMEDIATELY

Decide on an appropriate response to the behaviour — one which can be implemented immediately.

Sometimes that is all that is required. Some immediate responses may include:

IGNORE the child seeking your attention in inappropriate ways — react positively when the behaviour is appropriate.

BEHAVIOUR	**RESPONSE**
Miss Smith is conferencing with a small group of children; Jane calls out 'Mizz Smith, Mizz Smith, Mizz Smith, Mizz Smith. Ohh, ohh can I collect the lunches, Mizz Smith?...'	The teacher physically turns away from Jane and ignores the calling out.

COMMUNICATE POSITIVE EXPECTATIONS

Sophie races across the room to collect materials.	The teacher says, 'Sophie, we walk in our classroom.'

VERBALLY CORRECT — Use the child's name first to cue attention, thank the child for responding appropriately and cue appropriate behaviour i.e. using the stool.

Tommy is standing on his desk looking out of the window to see if it's stopped raining.	The teacher says 'Tommy, climb down from the desk. Thank you. If you want to see out of the window, use the foot stool.'

DISTRACT the child away from the situation.

Susan, a very volatile child, has her construction knocked down and is about to explode.	The teacher says 'Susan, let's pack these up together; then we can choose a book to read to the class'. The teacher might later say 'I understand you felt angry. Thank you for helping me to pack up'.

OFFER POSITIVE ALTERNATIVES to encourage appropriate behaviour.

Nguyen continues to draw with his special texta after everyone else has packed up.	The teacher says, 'Nguyen, you can either put your texta in your locker tray or in your school bag.'

AVOID CONFLICT which involves you in a power struggle with a child.

Cathy has been asked to line up for physical education. She crosses her arms and shouts 'NO! I'm staying here!'	The teacher says 'Okay, Cathy, we'll miss you, but when you feel ready come and join in'.

USE PEER MODELS which highlight appropriate behaviours. Note: choose a peer model that you know the child respects.

The class is moving to the library. Jimmy is running ahead, calling loudly back to the teacher.	The teacher says clearly, 'I like the way John is walking quietly and considering other classes'.

ACKNOWLEDGE POSITIVE behaviour when it occurs.

Jimmy stops running and rejoins the group.	➤ The teacher makes eye contact with Jimmy and smiles.

ENACT LOGICAL CONSEQUENCES which give choice to the child.

Jimmy continues to run ahead of the group towards the library.	➤ The teacher says, 'Jimmy, you can walk quietly with us to the library or spend library time working in Mr. Jackson's classroom — you decide.'

AVOID SIDETRACKING STRATEGIES — focus on one child's behaviour at a time.

'But Tommy called me a ... first', blustered Mark as he pointed at Tommy.	➤ The teacher moves and gains eye contact with Mark. She asserts, 'I'll deal with Tommy in a moment — but now, we're going to look at our problem.'

USE PHYSICAL RESTRAINT as a safety mechanism in order to protect people and property.

Tommy has pinned David to the floor and is punching him repeatedly in the face.	➤ The teacher moves quickly to Tommy, saying 'Tommy!' to try to gain his attention. (No response.) She physically restrains and moves him away from David.

NOTE: Physical restraint is only the first step in a response — it is *always* succeeded by constructive longer term strategies e.g. problem solving and logical consequences.

NEGOTIATE WITH CHILDREN

Accept that feelings are involved

Teacher: 'I feel so angry when Johnny wrecks others' work.'
'I can't stand Johnny when he's having one of his 'off' days.'
'I feel guilty after I've screamed at Johnny.'

Johnny: 'Mrs Jenkins picks on me all the time, I hate her.'
'It's always me that gets into trouble … sniff … sniff.'

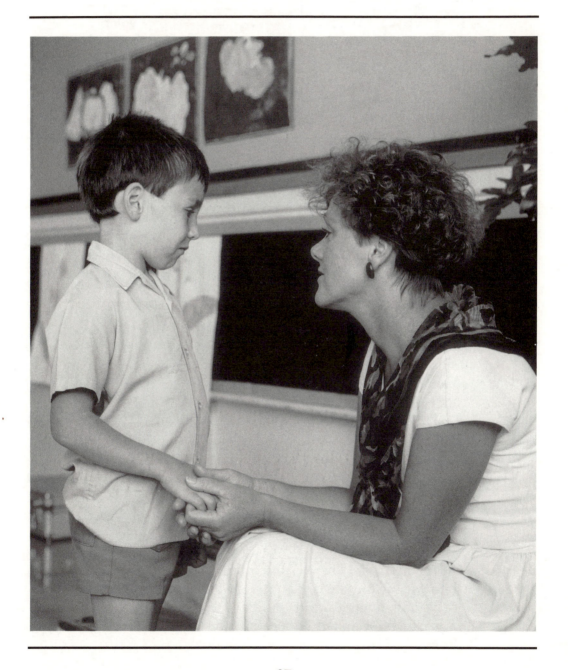

Interpersonal conflict arouses a range of emotions — it's part of being human. Recognise, though, that some of these feelings impede the effective resolution of conflict.

Choose a constructive time to negotiate

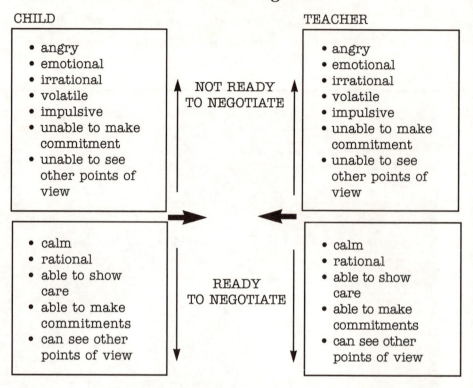

CHILD

TEACHER

- angry
- emotional
- irrational
- volatile
- impulsive
- unable to make commitment
- unable to see other points of view

NOT READY TO NEGOTIATE

- angry
- emotional
- irrational
- volatile
- impulsive
- unable to make commitment
- unable to see other points of view

- calm
- rational
- able to show care
- able to make commitments
- can see other points of view

READY TO NEGOTIATE

- calm
- rational
- able to show care
- able to make commitments
- can see other points of view

The best time for negotiation to occur is when all concerned can listen, think rationally and talk calmly. Take control of the situation by deciding when is the best time to negotiate — the handling of conflict and misbehaviour can often benefit from a time delay:

'Alice, I'm too angry to talk about this now. We'll deal with it later when I've calmed down.'

'Boys, I don't think you're ready to talk sensibly about this right now. Sit in those two spaces and think about what you did — I'll come back in five minutes.

Work on the problem together

Use a problem solving strategy which gives children, through negotiation, the chance to learn to accept responsibility for their behaviour, and to share in (and ultimately take control of) decision making towards problem solution. This can take place at a personal teacher-child level, in a small group setting, or at class level.

A PROCESS FOR MEETING BEHAVIOURAL NEEDS:

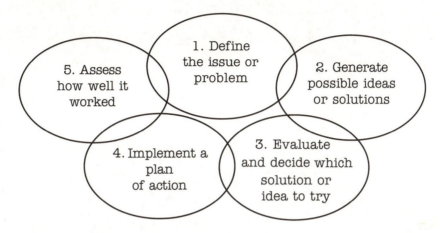

5. Assess how well it worked

1. Define the issue or problem

2. Generate possible ideas or solutions

4. Implement a plan of action

3. Evaluate and decide which solution or idea to try

Step 1: Define the problem

'Let's get the problem clear in both our minds so that we can work on it.'

'We've got a problem here, Johnny ...'

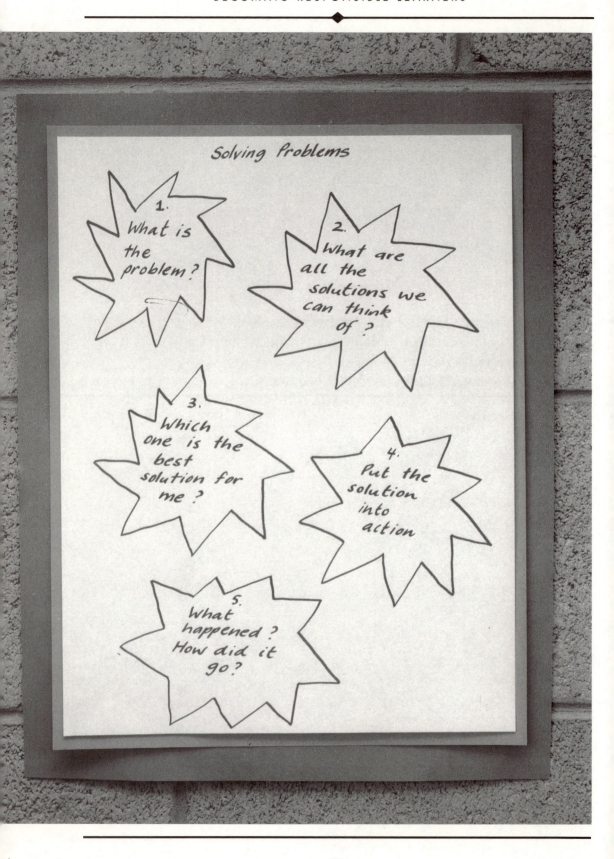

Solving Problems

1. What is the problem?

2. What are all the solutions we can think of?

3. Which one is the best solution for me?

4. Put the solution into action

5. What happened? How did it go?

'What did you do ...?'
'I didn't do nothing!'
'This is what I saw happening ...'

Give children as much help as needed at any step of the
process.

In this critical first step:
• focus on the behaviour.
• deal with one problem at a time.
• avoid being sidetracked.

Step 2: Generate possible solutions

'What can you do about it?'
'How can I help you?'
'How about this idea?'
Child: 'I can't ask her ... that's a dumb idea.'
Teacher: 'At this stage let's consider all ideas.'

Generate, don't evaluate at this stage!

Step 3: Evaluate and decide which solution can be used

'We've thought of lots of ideas — which ones do you think might
work?'
'What things will help us judge which ideas are best?'
'Which of these ideas would you like to try? Tony likes that idea
— how do you feel about it Pat?'
Child: 'I don't like any of them.'
Teacher: 'Okay well let's go back and think of some more ideas.'

Go back to previous steps where necessary.

Step 4: Implement a plan of action

'Okay then, we'll start tomorrow, and we'll see how well it's
worked at the end of the day.'
'Let's plan it carefully now — what will you need to do first?'
'Close your eyes ... imagine yourself doing it now ... tell me what
you can see happening.'

Make sure that the plan is clear and able to be achieved.

Step 5: Assess how well it worked

'Well, how did we go Rachel?'

'Rachel, you were able to follow your plan through — well done!'

'What else do you think you need to work on?'

> Provide feedback to the child, and opportunity for child self-assessment.

During problem solving:

- Focus on the behaviour, not the child.
  'These are the things you haven't finished today Mary' rather than 'You've been very lazy today Mary.'

- Be assertive rather than aggressive.

- Set realistic time lines — some problems are solved quickly, others require long-term sustained effort.

- Change language from 'we' to 'you' as children are ready to assume control.

CONTRACT FOR CHANGE

A contract is a two-way commitment which in this context makes explicit the behaviour change. It assumes that negotiation and problem solving have taken place.

Plan together

Review the agreed 'plan of action' (refer Step 4 of the Problem Solving Process, p. 39). 'Let's go over what we've agreed to try. I'll make sure … so, that's what I have to do. What is it you've agreed to do?'

Consider writing the plan down

Just as concrete materials help children in their academic learning, so too, they can help children learn how to behave appropriately. A visible contract helps in two ways:
- it acts as a concrete reminder of commitment made, and
- by physically accepting a contract, children are helped to accept responsibility for behaviour.

A PERSONAL CONTRACT FOR KYLIE

The classroom context: When children move to begin their learning challenges Kylie ignores these, zooms straight to the sink and starts her own waterplay. This occurs every day, and so her workjobs are not being done.

Contract for **Kylie**

1. Listen to the tape

2. Do the number jigsaw

3. Work with me

Miss Griggs

What does Kylie need to *learn* to do?

Although Kylie's teacher feels there are a number of things Kylie needs to learn, she wisely selects only one that both she and Kylie agree is critical to learn first — that of doing *a* learning challenge. Kylie has limited reading skills, and so a pictorial contract is appropriate here.

Keep the contract short

For a contract to be useful, it should say, in the shortest and clearest possible way, what we understand has been agreed to:

CONTRACT

I, Mr Cameron, will sit with David and explain his workjobs before he starts them.

I, David, will finish 3 workjobs today. We will meet during conference time (11.30am) and see how we're going.

Bill Cameron   David Donaldson

Give the contract to all parties concerned

'David, please take this now to Mrs Jones and get a copy made — that way, we'll each have our own.'

Keep contracts in a special place

'I'll keep my copy in the front of my work programme so that it won't get lost.'

'I'll sticky-tape mine in the front of my work folder — it will help me remember what to do.'

Contracts have different contexts. In this section we have focused on the classroom context, and so have involved teacher and child. However, it's important to include those who have a major influence on the behaviour. Where the behaviour is a school level issue, or a home-school issue, it may be necessary to involve senior staff, parents, principal, and so on.

APPLY CONSISTENT CONSEQUENCES

Children learn through both observing and experiencing the consequences of behaviour. In order to learn responsibility for behaviour, children need the choice of behaviours, along with their consequences, made explicit for them. These consequences must be manageable and able to be applied consistently.

Use consistent language and speak calmly

Use the child's name first as a cue. State the behaviour, offer a limited choice and their consequences.

'Tony, you're swearing in our classroom. You can choose to stop swearing and share good ideas with the rest of us, or you can move to that chair and we will do it without you.'

'Jason, you're not doing your work. You can do it now, or you can choose to spend some time doing it when it's playtime.'

Relate consequences logically
Consider the difference between these two examples.

'Belinda, you can pack up now and hear our story, or pack up during story time and miss hearing it!'
Reaction from child: 'That makes sense.'

'Belinda, if you don't pack up now you can miss out on Phys. Ed. tomorrow.'
Reaction from child: 'I hate her.'

Apply consequences consistently
'Thank you for packing up Belinda. Now we're all ready to hear our story.'

> Ensure positive feedback is given when appropriate choice is made.

'No, Belinda. This story is for people who've packed up. You'll have to miss out this time.'

> Follow through assertively and calmly when inappropriate choice is made.

Use withdrawal constructively
Withdrawal can be a type of logical consequence, and occurs only after a choice has been given. Withdrawal can be a constructive learning experience:

• when it offers the opportunity to think, to reflect, to observe

• when it allows people to calm down

• when it is seen as the *beginning* of a problem-solving process.

'What did I hope to achieve?'
'Where will the child be?'
'What does the child need to do while there?'
'When or how may the child return to the group?'

Some purposes of withdrawal.

I need to separate these two so they can get their work done.	• Move the child to another working space in the classroom: 'Toni you are touching Kristy's work. Come and sit over here until you've finished your work.'
Sandra needs time to calm down.	• Move the child to a place in class, which has been designated 'for being by myself'. The child decides when she is ready to rejoin the group: 'Sandra, you hit John with the ruler. Sit here until you feel ready to join back in.'
Jack needs to learn how to share materials.	• Move the child to a 'special' place in class to observe and reflect: 'Jack, you weren't sharing the paints as we agreed you would do. Sit on the chair — look at what the people who are painting are doing. I'll be back in a moment and we'll talk about what you've noticed.'
Sandra has now chosen twice not to work with John. I'll need to set aside some time and do some further problem solving with her.	• Move the child to a 'special' place in the classroom for a set period: 'Sandra, you hit John again. Sit in the 'by myself' space for 5 minutes (egg timer) — then come and see me and we'll discuss it.'
This child's driving me batty! I've tried everything! It looks like the plan Glenda and I decided on is about to be tried. On-going problem-solving is going to be important here.	• Move the child to a special supervised place outside the classroom: 'Peter, we've talked about this before. No-one can hear in our room when you make that noise. You can choose to stop the noise and work with us, or you can work with Mrs Graham for the rest of the morning.'

Consequences are *not* punishments — they are related to the child's choice. Consequences assert that the child is responsible for their behaviour, not the teacher.

MAKE TIME TO BUILD RELATIONSHIPS

Use people from outside the classroom to support the class while you are working with the child individually or in a small group

'Rather than Mrs Graham working with Tony, she takes other groups while I work with Tony or Tony's group. I find I'm building better rapport with Tony.'

Help parents to be an effective resource

'That after-school parent workshop on reading has really paid off! I have three regular parent helpers who work effectively with small groups — it means I can use my time to meet individual needs.'

Use conferencing time flexibly

'It's just as important to use conferencing time to discuss behaviour and do some problem-solving as it is to discuss curriculum issues.'

ENLIST PEER SUPPORT

Use the peer group context — it can be the most powerful agent of positive change in the classroom

> Sophie often makes odd noises during quiet working or listening times. Mr Anderson initially ignores these, with little success, since children are providing positive feedback to Sophie by laughing and giggling. Mr Anderson talks with the class and they all agreed to ignore Sophie when she makes these noises. As Sophie's audience 'disappears', so do the noises.

Encourage positive peer feedback

> Mr Anderson says to Jane at lunchtime, 'Thank you for ignoring Sophie's noises when you were working next to her this morning. That was really helpful.'
>
> > Give children positive feedback when they have been supportive.

Kate, overhearing this, says, 'Yeah, we were able to hear better because it was quiet.' Mr Anderson smiles and replies 'Perhaps you would like to tell Sophie how helpful she was.'

Encourage peers to give each other positive feedback.

Make use of problem solving in small groups

When difficulties arise in a small group setting, use the process outlined on p. 39 to help the group deal with the problem.

'It's my job to help the group deal with its own problems, rather than solve their problems for them. I'm not only modelling steps in the problem-solving process, but I'm gradually making kids aware of what these steps are.'

Hold regular class meetings

• Use it as a problem solving forum, using the process on p. 39.

Class Meeting Rules.

1. Only one person speaks at a time.

2. Put your hand up to speak.

3. No put downs.

4. Be sensible.

5. If it's said in here, it stays in here.

- Problems may be child or teacher introduced:
  'Some people in our classroom are having trouble coming in on time after the bell has gone. What have other people noticed?' (teacher-introduced problem)
  'What things, if any, would you like to talk about today?'
  'Someone's stealing my lunch.' (child-introduced problem)
- Have fun as a group, too:
  'Phew! We've done some hard work on that problem. Let's leave it there, and go outside for a game.'

Effective teachers seem to approach learning and behaviour challenges in similar ways. They acknowledge the strong links between learning and behaviour and use consistent processes for both. (Refer Problem-Solving Process, p. 62). Importantly, they share the secret with children by making explicit what those processes are.

4

SHARING RESPONSIBILITY AT SCHOOL LEVEL

Working with children who have behaviour difficulties can be very stressful and is often a task that is too big for any one person. Teachers with such children in their classrooms see the following kinds of support as valuable:

- a shared approach to problem solving when classroom resources alone are not appropriate for behaviour change

- procedures which are consistent and known across the school

- school structures that provide opportunities for team-building and peer support

- a school commitment to ongoing learning.

SHARE THE PROBLEM WITH OTHERS

All people who have major influence on changing the child's behaviour should be involved at some stage in the problem solving process. Without this involvement, little positive change will occur. A critical first step is to decide whose problem the behaviour is.

Consider these situations:

During movement sessions, Garry constantly giggles, probes and pinches others, and refuses to participate. Mrs Saunders has consistently applied the consequences of his behaviour, including sitting-out the activities and observing others. It's reached the stage where the class can't effectively do movement with Garry there.

'Whose problem is this?' Mrs Saunders thinks, 'It's gone beyond the classroom — who needs to be involved?'

Mrs Saunders and Miss Allen, a senior staff member, agreed that it would be most undesirable to deprive the class of movement sessions. Together they planned for Miss Allen to supervise Garry during movement times until Garry, Mrs Saunders and Miss Allen worked out a way for Garry to participate.

Mr Roberts catches up with Mrs Saunders at the end of playtime — 'Tanya's been fighting in the playground again — you're her classroom teacher. What do you think we ought to do?' They briefly discuss what happened and agree that Tanya has broken a *school* understanding on playground behaviour, and therefore the appropriate person to deal with the incident is Miss Allen, a senior member of staff.

Craig spends playtimes alone watching other children. In class, it's difficult to get him involved in learning activities. Miss Montelli is concerned and is unsure how best to help Craig. After talking with the principal, a meeting is set up with Craig's parents, Miss Montelli and a guidance officer. Information-sharing reveals that Craig's oldest brother died suddenly six months ago. Community support agencies for the family were discussed, and strategies planned to assist Craig at school.

Although the situations differ, the approach used had features in common. Two important decisions need to be made *before* the problem-solving process is implemented.

Who has the problem? or Whose rule has been broken?	school? community? classroom?
Who needs to be involved to help?	child/children? parents? senior staff? principal? class teacher? outside consultant? regional administrator?

DEVELOP POLICY ON PUPIL WELFARE

A policy collaboratively developed by staff, children and parents has several important benefits:

- it makes explicit a common set of expectations

- it offers consistent procedures to follow

- it offers the opportunity to reflect and plan in *proactive* ways, rather than simply reacting as crises occur

- there is likely to be greater support and commitment to making the policy work.

All of these are critical factors towards helping children with behaviour difficulties.

Some teachers may ask, 'If they want us to have a policy on pupil welfare, why don't they just give us one?'

The content of any policy document is important and we have seen many excellent examples in schools. What makes the difference though, between a policy that gathers dust on shelves and a policy that is genuinely enacted, is the *way* in which people have been involved in its development. Policy is more likely to be effective when all who are influenced by it are involved in its formulation — teachers, children and the parent community. Processes for achieving this vary, but any effective process will contain the following steps:

Step 1 Be aware of the need for policy

'We will have to do something about this fighting in the playground. It's happening too often.'
'Wouldn't it be good if we could be consistent with kids?'
'Let's bring this up at the staff meeting. We do need to talk about it.'

Step 2 Clarify Values

Spend time discussing individual values so that agreement can be reached on a *school* set of values.

'I find bad language offensive at any time.'

'I believe children should be able to use their home language in class, and swearing's part of that.'

> Agreed school value: We respect the child's home language, but expect children to use appropriate school language.

Step 3 Make a Plan

After clarifying values and gathering information so that school goals are clear, work out a plan for how those goals can be achieved.

'Now we know how we expect children to behave and we know how they expect us to behave, let's make a plan ...'

Step 4 Implement plan and review regularly

'Let's look at our goals and list some simple ways we might judge how successful we've been. We'll use these to help us review at the end of term.'

'Hey! Let's prepare a survey for the kids to fill in.'

'Well, one yardstick would be that we all make a commitment to work on it... another... we could do some playground observations.'

WORK CO-OPERATIVELY WITH COLLEAGUES

Teaching can be a profession where it is easy to feel alone and be left alone — especially when one is struggling to cope. Working with peers has two key benefits — it provides practical, positive support, and serves as a powerful forum for effective learning to take place.

lessens feelings
of isolation

decreases
teacher stress

shares
responsibility

provides a forum
for frustrations

builds a
positive climate

PEER
SUPPORT

PEER
LEARNING

shares ideas
successes
problems

provides
modelling

offers on-site
assistance

provides
on-going learning

increases
professionalism

58

Make time to be with peers

School leadership which spends time team-building in informal ways is well placed to develop a constructive climate for peer support and professional learning in more formal settings. Effective teachers value:

- early opportunities to meet new members of staff and mix in social settings
- the chance to regularly talk with other *adults*
- the opportunity to get to know both peers and senior staff at a more personal level.

Make time to work with peers

Peers can have a greater influence on our learning and professional growth than any outside person or 'package'. Effective teachers have found the following strategies useful:

- Working with a trusted colleague to observe and give feedback on areas of specific focus in each other's classroom:

  'I'm trying a new way of responding to interruptions. When you come in this morning could you make some observations?'

'I noticed you ignored interruptions and rewarded those who had their hands up. Is there something we can add to the strategy that will stop interruptions altogether?'

● Working with one or more colleagues to plan jointly and evaluate programming for children:
'At our school, we've structured our timetable so that teacher teams have off-class time together to plan.'

● Team-Teaching:
'When you come in today, can you take the rest of the class so that I can do some really intensive work with Rachel?'

● Forming one or more support networks in the school which provide a forum for small groups of teachers to share ideas, concerns, and problem-solve together.

Peer support groups should:
• be voluntary
• meet regularly
• focus on the needs of the people in them
• offer positive practical support

Make a commitment to ongoing learning

Teachers today face increasingly complex challenges and demands, both inside and outside their classrooms. Schools which help teachers to meet these challenges are those that view professional development as critical to their ongoing growth.

Professional development which fosters ongoing learning:
● is seen as a process, rather than a series of 'one off' activities
● is collaborative in planning and implementation
● involves teachers in planning, acting and reflecting i.e. action research in their classrooms
● helps teachers to reflect on their practices and to develop new knowledge and skills
● promotes teaming, and networking between schools
● provides ongoing consultancy support.*

---

* School Curriculum and Organisation Framework, P-12, Ministry of Education (Schools Division), Victoria, 1988.

5

A PROBLEM–SOLVING
PROCESS

'Now that we've agreed we want to find out some things about milk cartons,' Helen says to her Year 1/2 children, 'let's think about all the things we already know.'

Together they brainstorm and Helen writes their ideas down on the blackboard.

'We've certainly found a lot,' says Helen. 'If these are all the things we know, what are the sorts of things we would like to find out?'

Through discussion with children, a list of nine learning challenges results.

'Let's look at these challenges one at a time' says Helen, 'and think of ways we might explore each one.' The children talk about a range of different ways they might approach the learning challenges. Since the class will be working in pairs, Helen asks them to think about which challenge they would like to explore with their partner and allows a brief time for decision making.

'Now that you've decided,' says Helen, 'talk through your plan with each other. Agree on an approach and think about things like how you'll manage your time through the week, what materials you'll need, where you might work on the challenge you've chosen, and how you'll work together.'

Children in pairs spend five minutes talking through their initial plan.

'O.K.,' says Helen, 'remember, our class goal is to find out lots of things about milk cartons! How will we know and show that we've been successful?'

Children establish two simple criteria which Helen writes on the board:

- Each partner will do a fair share of the work.
- By Friday pairs will be ready to share with everyone the things they've learned.

Children eagerly set to work collecting materials and moving to different parts of the room to pursue the science challenge they had chosen.

Things proceed smoothly and Helen works with various pairs, until a few minutes before lunch when chaos arises at the sink in the wet area. Three pairs have wanted to explore the waterproof properties of milk cartons at the one time. Helen moves to the children at the sink asking them, 'What's the problem here?' to which various children reply 'We were here first', and 'We can't fit at the sink all at once', and 'There's water everywhere because we're trying to fit our cartons in the sink'.

'Well,' says Helen, 'are you saying there are too many children at the sink at one time?'

'Yes,' chorus the children.

'What are the things you can do about it?' asks Helen. 'Let's think of some ideas.'

'We could bring in a bucket of water and some people could use that,' suggests Fiona.

'Or,' says James, 'we could just let the people work here who were here first.'

'We could have a roster like we do with our computer,' suggests Matthew.

'Or we could just ban everybody from the sink,' says Tameka.

'You've just thought of several ideas,' asserts Helen, 'Which of these ideas do you think might work?'

'If we ban everyone,' says Matthew, 'no-one would get a turn and that wouldn't be fair.'

'And it wouldn't be fair if only the people there first had a go,' complains Tameka.

'You seem to be saying that being fair to everybody is important,' comments Helen. 'Which of the ideas then do you think might work and be fair to everybody?'

Following brief discussion the children agree to draw up a roster, with a set time for each pair. After helping them to prepare their plan, Helen says, 'It's almost lunch time now, let's start tomorrow and we'll see how it has worked …'

The next day Helen follows up with the group asking, 'How did you go with your roster this morning, what worked well, what needs changing …?'

On Friday, after pairs had shared their learnings with everybody, Helen says, 'Let's think some more about the learning we've been doing this week — remember when we had that trouble at the sink the other day — what was happening?'

'There was a problem because there were too many people at the sink,' says Mia.

'So, the first thing we had to do was decide on what the problem was,' Helen says, writing '1 Decide on the problem' on the board.

'What did we have to do then?' she asks.

'You made us think of ideas for solving the problem,' supplies Matthew.

Accordingly, Helen writes, '2 Think of ideas for solving the problem'.

Through further discussion with children, Helen draws from them the next of the steps in the problem solving process, and using child language adds them to the list on the board:

1 Decide on the problem.
2 Think of ideas for solving the problem.
3 Decide which idea might work.
4 Plan how to do it and do it.
5 Reflect on how it went.

'O.K.,' says Helen, 'they're the steps we went through in solving that problem. Where else might you be able to use these steps to help you solve problems?'

Children make various suggestions and suddenly Mia sits up and exclaims, 'Miss Fox, that's sort of like what we've done in science this week!'

'It is, isn't it,' smiles Helen. 'You've just made a very important connection — let's talk about it some more …'

Helen acknowledges the powerful links between learning and behaviour. She helps children to see these links by modelling consistent processes in various contexts, and makes them explicit by having children reflect on their learning.

Helen, and other successful teachers like her, recognise that, just as science and other areas of the curriculum are learned, so, too, is behaviour. Just as children need opportunities to explore, practise and make mistakes in academic learning, so, too, they need opportunities to explore, practise and make mistakes in learning appropriate ways to behave. An important process which gives children the opportunity to learn responsibility for both their learning and behaviour is the one that Helen used:

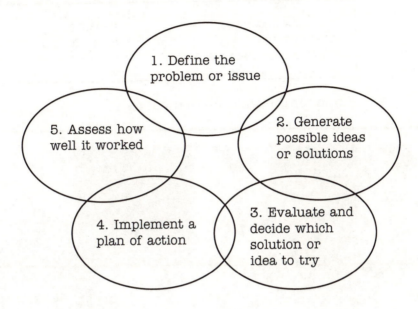

It is a consistent process for both learning and behaviour

Define the issue or problem.

'What do we know?'

'What are the things we need to know?'

'We've got a problem here ... let's get it clear in both our minds so that we can work on it.'

Generate possible solutions/alternative ideas.

'What are all the ways we might explore that?'

'What ideas might help you?'

'What are the things you can do about it?'

Evaluate and decide which solution/idea is best.

'Which question will you choose to explore?'

'Which of these ideas do you think might work?'

Implement a plan of action.

'How will we go about finding out?'

'Let's plan it out — what will you need to do first?'

'Let's start tomorrow and we'll see how it has worked ...'

Assess how well it worked.

'How will we know and show that we've been successful?'

'How did you go? Which part did you do well?'

'What do you need to work on?'

Use with:

individual children	parents
small groups	colleagues
whole class meetings	

Empower the children to use it too.

The Making of Powerful Learners

There is one belief underlying all of the key strategies we have shared:

Children can learn to take responsibility for both their behaviour and their learning.

Effective teachers communicate this belief by the way they work at:

- being assertive with children
- staying calm, positive and consistent
- retaining a sense of humour
- building positive relationships with children
- negotiating rather than setting up 'win-lose' situations
- focusing on pro-active learning and teaching strategies
- using peer support structures
- being on-going learners.

Such teachers acknowledge that there are no 'quick-fix' solutions to helping children with behaviour difficulties. They know that meaningful and constructive change can only be guaranteed when people learn to take increasing control of themselves. And perhaps most of all, they know that children *can* learn to do this.

RECOMMENDED READING

Balson, M. (1982) *Understanding Classroom Behaviour.* A.C.E.R., Burnley (Victoria).

Cowan, M.; Freeman, L.; Farmer, A.; James, M.; Drent, A. & Arthur, R. (1985) *Positive School Discipline: A Practical Guide to Developing Policy.* Parents and Friends of Monnington Publications, Melbourne.

Dalton, J. (1985) *Adventures in Thinking: Creative Thinking and Co-operative Talk in Small Groups.* Nelson, Melbourne.

Glasser, W. (1986) *Control Theory in the Classroom.* Harper & Row, N.Y.

Hill, S. & Hill, T. (1990) *The Collaborative Classroom: A Guide to Co-operative Learning.* Eleanor Curtain, Melbourne.

Wolfgang, C.H. & Glickman, C.D. (1986) *Solving Discipline Problems: Strategies for Classroom Teachers.* 2nd Ed. Allyn and Bacon, Sydney.